How to
Think More
Effectively

How to
Think More
Effectively

The School of Life

Published in 2020 by The School of Life
930 High Road, London, N12 9RT
First published in the USA in 2020

Designed and typeset by Marcia Mihotich
Printed in Latvia by Livonia Print

A proportion of this book has appeared online at
www.theschooloflife.com/articles

Every effort has been made to contact the copyright holders of the
material reproduced in this book. If any have been inadvertently
overlooked, the publisher will be pleased to make restitution at the
earliest opportunity.

The School of Life publishes a range of books on essential topics in
psychological and emotional life, including relationships, parenting,
friendship, careers and fulfilment. The aim is always to help us to
understand ourselves better – and thereby to grow calmer, less confused
and more purposeful. Discover our full range of titles, including books
for children, here:
www.theschooloflife.com/books

The School of Life also offers a comprehensive therapy service, which
complements, and draws upon, our published works:
www.theschooloflife.com/therapy

www.theschooloflife.com

ISBN 978-1-912891-13-9

10 9 8 7 6

Introduction

One of the odder aspects of our minds is how variable they are in the quality of their output. At certain moments, we are capable of great insight and creativity; at others, everything that emerges from us feels leaden, earthbound and clichéd. Although the good progress of our lives depends on our minds functioning at their peak, we don't generally suppose that there is much we could do to control or influence the quality of our thoughts. In fallow periods, we tend to hope that letting time pass will improve matters. We see good thinking in mystical terms: as a gift from outside forces that we cannot steer or regulate.

However, we need not be so pessimistic: we can learn to improve our chances of having good thoughts by paying closer attention to the operation of our minds and by practising mental manoeuvres designed to tease the best out of them. We can more systematically observe what happens when we are on a rewarding track and learn to jog ourselves onto one through deft exercises of the will and the imagination.

We should not be surprised that we are so unpractised in this area. Our societies pay enormous attention to the results of good thinking but very little to their genesis. Our education systems operate with a narrow sense of what fruitful thinking involves; the focus is on facts and formulae, on the capacity to reel off quotes and summarise opposing views.

We are taught to obsess about passing exams: that is, trials marked by people who feel confident that they already know the existing truths and are merely checking whether we have learnt to submit to them too. School thinking marks us for life and lends us an ongoing bias towards neglecting our individual perceptions in favour of meeting pre-existing expectations. But genuine adult achievement relies on a capacity for originality and authenticity of thought. Effective thinking isn't about 'working hard' in any brute or rote sense; it is about learning to spot, defend, nurture and grow our fleeting, tentative periods of insight.

What follows are a set of moves that hope to release the better parts of our minds and to help us identify and hold on to our prime mental moments. The suggestion on offer is that we can learn systematically to harvest rather than sporadically to forage our most satisfying and necessary thoughts.

1
Strategic Thinking

There is a fundamental distinction to be made between two kinds of thinking: figuring out what we would like to achieve, and working out how to achieve it. Put another way, there is a key difference between *strategy* on the one hand and *execution* on the other. Strategy is about determining our overall aims; execution comprises everything that follows once we've decided – the practical activities required to put our plans into action.

It is natural to assume that we would spend a lot of time on strategy before we turned our attention to execution – however successful we might be in carrying out our plans, what really counts is having the right plans to work from in the first place. Our results can only be as good as the aims that first led to them.

But there is a paradoxical aspect to the way our minds operate: as a general rule, we're much better at execution than at strategy. We appear to have an innate energy for working through obstacles to our goals and an equally innate resistance to pausing to understand what these goals should rightly be. We seem to be as lackadaisical about strategy as we are assiduous about execution.

We see the outcome of this bias across many areas. We concentrate more on making money than on figuring out how to spend it optimally. We put a lot more effort into becoming 'successful' than into assessing how dominant notions of success could make us content. At a collective level, corporations are much more committed to the efficient delivery of their existing products and services than on stepping back and asking afresh what the company might truly be trying to do for their customers. Nations are more concerned with growing their GDP than with probing at the benefits of increased purchasing power. Humanity is vastly better at engineering than philosophy: our planes are a good deal more impressive than our notions of what we should travel for; our abilities to communicate definitively outstrip our ideas of how to understand one another.

In every case, we prefer to zero in on the mechanics, on the means and the tools rather than on the guiding question of ends. We are almost allergic to the large first-order enquiries: what are we ultimately trying to do here? What would best serve our happiness? Why should we bother? How is this aligned with real value?

There are tragic consequences to this over-devotion to execution. We rush frantically to fulfil hastily chosen ends; we exhaust ourselves blindly in the name of sketchy goals; we chain ourselves to schedules, timelines and performance targets. All the while, we avoid asking what we might really need in order to flourish and so frequently learn, at the end of a lifetime of superhuman effort, that we had the wrong destinations from the start.

Perhaps it should not surprise us that our minds have such a pronounced bias towards executive labour over strategic reflection. From an evolutionary perspective, mulling over strategic questions was never a high priority. For most of history, the strategic goals would have been obvious: to find sufficient things to eat, to reproduce, to get through the winter and to keep the tribe safe from attack. Execution was where all the urgent and genuine difficulties lay: how to light a fire in wet weather; how to make sharper arrowheads; where to find wild strawberries or the right leaves to calm down an inflammation. We are the descendants of generations that made a succession of complex discoveries in the service of a few basic goals. Only in the conditions of modernity – where we are surrounded by acute choices as to what to do with our lives and when our aim is happiness rather than basic survival – have strategic questions become at once necessary and costly to avoid.

Little about our formal education has prepared us for this development. At school, 'working hard' still means dutifully following the curriculum, not wondering whether it happens to be correct. 'Why should we study this subject?' sounds, to most teachers, like an insult and a provocation, rather than the birth of an admirably speculative mindset. Once we start employment, most companies want the bulk of their employees to execute orders rather than reflect on their validity. We might be reaching middle age before we are granted the first formal incentives to think strategically.

Even in daily life, raising strategic questions can feel tiresome and odd. To ask 'what's the point of doing this?' is easy to mistake for a piece of provocative negativity. If we challenge our acquaintances with any degree of seriousness with questions such as: 'What is a good holiday?', 'What is a relationship *for*?', 'What is a satisfying conversation?' or 'Why do we want money?', we risk coming across as absurd and pretentious – as though such large questions were by definition unanswerable.

The real dangers lie in never daring to raise such questions. We already possess fragmentary, disorganised but important information that could help us to make progress with the larger strategic dilemmas. We have already been on a sufficient number of holidays and shopping trips; we have already had some relationships and been through a number of career shifts; we have had a chance to observe the connections between what we do and how we feel. Therefore, at least in theory, we have gathered the necessary material from which to draw rich conclusions as to our happiness and our purpose, as to meaning and the right human ends. We have the data; the challenge is to process it by running it through the sieve of the larger questions.

We should dare to move the emphasis of our thinking away from execution and towards strategy.

Mental Manoeuvre

1. An immediate step is to grow more conscious of the way we presently spend our time: we might be devoting 95% of our waking hours to execution and a mere 5% to strategy. Acknowledging the unfair bias, we should strive to ensure that at least 20% of our efforts is henceforth devoted to reflecting on the deeper 'why' questions before we allow ourselves to 'relax' into the more familiar and more routine work of execution.

2. We should observe how often and how naturally we devote our time to executing our ideas before we have submitted them to adequate scrutiny. We should note our discomfort around questions like: Why is this a worthwhile effort? Where will I be in a few years if this goes right? How is this connected with what fulfils me? What is the point here? We should watch our comparative enthusiasm for launching ourselves into projects in a hurry, for fretting only about the lower-level procedural hiccups and for ensuring that we are too 'busy' ever to leave time for reflection. We should grow suspicious of our covert devotion to rush over enquiry.

3. To accompany us in this, we need to redraw where prestige is accorded, to downgrade the glamour that presently clings to frantic busy-ness and to raise, to a corresponding degree, the image of speculative reflection. We need a new collective sense of what

hard work might involve and even what it might look like. It won't necessarily be the person who runs from meeting to meeting or juggles international phone calls who is genuinely engaged in working hard; it might be the person sitting at the window, gazing out at the clouds, occasionally cupping their head in their hands and writing something down in a little notebook.

Who is really working?

4. We need support with how uncomfortable strategic thinking can feel. We need to be reassured that we aren't unusually wicked or flighty to be tempted to act rather than think, and should forgive ourselves for the strength of our wish to avoid all large first-order questions. We need encouragement to stick at probing the point and the meaning even when the overwhelming desire is to bury ourselves in correspondence or scan the news. We need to notice how oddly and humblingly lazy we are where it really counts.

Why is strategic thinking so hard?

In the Middle Ages, it was widely agreed that the most important thing to think about was God. Today, the subject most of us have to focus our attention on is our purpose. But in the Middle Ages, leading figures were prepared to accept that prolonged non-distracted attention was an arduous demand to make of our inherently fragile and wayward psyches. They knew how much our minds long to flee themselves, and realised that one might need to institute some dramatic-looking steps to help us to keep our focus. One of these important moves was the invention of the monastery.

The monastery made a range of extreme-sounding innovations in the arena of non-distraction. It proposed that, to keep the mind clear, one might need to live far removed from towns and cities, usually on the side of a mountain or cliff or in a sparsely inhabited stretch of countryside. As a continual reminder of the importance of thinking, the architecture would have to be solemn, grand and imposing. The walls were to be high and thick without many doors or picture windows giving out onto the wider world.

There might need to be secluded courtyards and inner fountains to calm the mind with the sound of trickling water. Bedrooms would have to be sparse, equipped only with a bed and a desk – but still uplifting and well constructed.

Medieval Christianity developed rules about how to live in monastic buildings. One of the earliest and most influential rule-setters was a Roman nobleman living at the end of the 5th century by the name of Benedict. He founded a number of monasteries in Italy and wrote an instruction manual for his followers, with a simple and emphatic title: *The Rule*. The prescriptions inside were beautifully precise and bold. They included thoughts on the following topics:

Eating

Rule 39: Except the sick who are very weak, let all abstain entirely from eating the flesh of four-footed animals.

One was to consume modest but nutritious meals only twice a day. Lamb and beef were to be avoided for their tendencies to bring on sleepiness, but chicken and fish in small quantities were deemed helpful. During meals, people were not allowed to talk to one another but were to listen to someone reading from an important and interesting book. If they needed something, they were to make a signal with their hands.

Silence

One needed to be quiet for most of the day and was allowed to talk only in certain places and at certain times. Gossip and malicious comments were forbidden, because they could be so absorbing.

Hair and clothing

To avoid distraction, one needed to wear clothes that were the same as those of everyone else in the community: something plain and useful. Not too expensive. And, so as to stop one fiddling with one's hair, it was deemed best for it all to be shorn off.

Fra Angelico, *Crucifixion
with Saints (detail: head of
St. Benedict)*, 1441

Exercise

Rule 35: Let the brethren serve one another, and let no one be excused from the kitchen service except by reason of sickness.

If one was going to be concentrating a lot on ideas and intellectual activities, it was thought wise to perform some physical activity every day; something repetitive and soothing such as sweeping the floor or weeding a row of lettuces.

Routine

One was to go to bed early and get up early. Routine was crucial. One would be doing the same thing at the same time day after day.

Sex

Everyone was to dress and behave demurely. Sex was known to play havoc with attempts to concentrate.

Art

At many strategic points in the buildings, one would see beautiful or dramatic works of art that reminded one of the significance of one's reflections.

Today, we are unlikely to be preoccupied with ridding ourselves of distraction in the name of our relationship with God. It is around the examination of our goals that the issue of distraction arises: we constantly feel the tug of a daydream, of a speculation about where someone obtained a certain pair of shoes or headphones, or a concern

Monk's cell, San Marco
Monastery, Florence, 1442
(on the wall, Fra Angelico's
Annunciation).

with the annoying way one's hair is falling at the back. With the example of St Benedict in mind, one could imagine a number of steps to end the tragic dominance of distraction and support strategic thinking:

Diet
Meticulous attention to the impact of what one eats on how one thinks. An emphasis on vegetables (especially aubergine and broccoli) and, perhaps, on the lighter kinds of fish.

Office uniforms
Ideally elegant but modest enough to dampen libidinous thoughts.

Physical exercise
Brief doses of gardening or maintenance work between periods of reflection.

A ban on the Internet
It could sound prudish, naive or dated, but it might be easier to admit that certain technologies simply outstrip our capacities for self-control.

Architecture
Tranquil and grand; facilities for periods of live-in work. Fewer open-plan offices. More cells.

_____ We should dare to move the emphasis of our thinking away from execution and towards strategy.

Art

Reminders of the nobility of reflective labour. Beautiful images of people thinking while gazing out of the window.

Monasteries stand as reminders of the fact that if we want to focus our minds on serious and difficult things, we may at points have to take some radical steps – and to do things that will strike some people as odd and or even unwarranted. Setting up the conditions for good thinking will itself require thought – which our societies have little interest in, because they have not yet properly admitted to themselves how big a grip distraction actually has on us – and how noble and important it remains to commit ourselves to regular periods of reflection. To think more effectively, we need to build ourselves monasteries of the mind.

2
Cumulative Thinking

The point is as basic as it is key: our minds do not disclose their more elaborate and best thoughts in one go. The mind is an intermittent instrument whose ideas come out in dribs and drabs. It is capable of a few inspired moves, then falls silent and needs to rest and to lie fallow for bewilderingly long periods. We cannot *think* for two hours at a stretch, let alone an entire day. The mind can't neatly follow office hours. One paragraph might be the work of a morning; an entire book of three slow years.

We tend to miss this when we encounter the thoughts of others. Because they frequently sound so composed and can be digested in an effortless stretch, we too readily imagine that these thoughts emerged in a coherent burst. We forget that a lakeful of ideas had to be pooled together with painful effort from spoonfuls of thinking arduously collected over long days and nights.

As a result, we are often dismayed at our own desultory first efforts. Our misfortune is to look always at the final results of the thinking efforts of others, while knowing our own efforts primarily from the inside. The contrast is so great that we tend to conclude that we are incapable of anything valuable rather than that we are – quite normally and understandably – stuck. We fail to draw courage from witnessing the struggles of those we admire. What alarms us is not so much how hard the task is but how easy we imagined it might be.

To calm us down and reassure us of the inevitability of humiliation, we should pay special attention not to the books but to the manuscripts of great thinkers. The French novelist Marcel Proust (1871–1922) reads as one of the most polished and fluent writers of

One of Proust's notebooks.

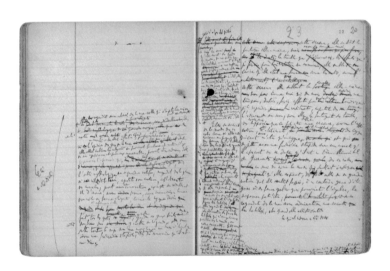

any age; his thoughts appear to flow ceaselessly from one point to the next. But his manuscripts suggest a different genesis. These densely packed notebooks are filled with multiple layers of changes, side notes, reminders, suggestions; sections moved about, crossed out, revised, abandoned, taken up again and ultimately rejected. The Proust we read is an artificial voice assembled over years, not spontaneously generated in the hours that are required to read him.

Whatever his genius, Proust was not unique in his process of mental assembly. We are all incapable of bringing the best of ourselves to the fore in any compact span of time. No single moment offers us the opportunity to consider an idea with complete adequacy or from a sufficient number of angles. We need time to pass so that we can return with a mindset imbued with multiple qualities.

At any single point, we are hemmed in in terms of what we can think by what we've just had to eat (as St Benedict knew, we'll be in a different mental state depending on whether we've had a veal escalope or some tomatoes in olive oil); the time of day (the way we think at 8 a.m. is utterly unlike the reflections of 11.30 p.m.); what we've recently been reading; the outlook of the people we've been around; the progress of our digestion; whether things have been going well or badly in a relationship, and the axis of the earth at the specific time of year (spring has its thoughts as well as its weathers). Each mental moment is favourable to certain ideas and pushes other potentially important insights into the background.

In order to carry off any moderately complicated thinking task, we should understand that, at any single moment, we won't have access to all the ideas we need. We'll have to set down what we can, then wait and return with the distinctive intelligence of a new mood.

What we witness in authors' jottings is a reminder of the delays we all have to endure before we can assemble ideas into the sequence that their underlying logic demands. When we have a more accurate picture of how our thinking processes work, we will have a more helpful perspective on the difficulty of what we're asking our brains to do. Instead of feeling that we must be fools for finding the task so hard, we will see that our troubles around building up our thoughts are not the result of any special failing on our part, but rather derive from the basic architecture of the mind. We have to counter this failing, as Proust did, with many stages of revision, addition, deletion and correction before we can arrive at the seemingly obvious, neat and clear final version. In every office or above every desk there should be an image from the messy early stages of a masterpiece to keep this basic, consoling and encouraging truth where it belongs: at the front of our sporadic, time-bound minds.

Mental Manoeuvre

1. The most necessary tool for thinking is also the simplest: the notebook. We need a notebook because we can't contain what is important within the bandwidth of active memory. We can't keep in view what is significant within our amnesiac, misty, temperamental consciousness. The paper has to function as a secondary memory to pool us together; it will end up knowing more of who we are than we can ourselves actively bring to mind in the moment.

2. On the notebook's pages, an idea from Monday morning in November will meet its logical counterpart, which will come to us only in January in the middle of a turbulent night. A vital parenthesis will enter the mind a year after an initial sentence.

3. Writing our thoughts down allows us to return to ideas when we have forgotten what we were trying to say and to see with greater clarity whether we have said it properly or not. We can remeet an idea 'cold', without the flattering energy of our initial enthusiasm, and so can perceive it as a less forgiving stranger might view it. We can note how much more work we need to do to let someone else understand what we are still, as yet, only meaning to say rather than actually saying. Our notebooks are the forum for a second, third and hundredth chance; they end up doing greater justice to our thoughts than our minds themselves.

3
Butterfly Thinking

One of the frustrating features of our minds is that the more interesting or pertinent our thoughts are, the more they have a tendency to escape our grasp. There seems to be a devilish correlation between how important and necessary a thought is to us and how likely it is to elude our command. The truly precious thoughts have something almost airborne about them, so inclined are they to flit away at the slightest approach of our conscious selves.

Many of the world's finest thinkers have equated ideas with winged creatures. The ancient Greek philosopher Plato (b. 429 BCE) compared the mind to a large cage in which a number of birds – or ideas – are circulating. He added that we can only catch these birds when they are sitting on a perch, but they spend much of their time agitatedly racing from one end of the cage to the other, leaving only a blur of feathers. Great ideas may pass *through* our minds, yet, as Plato knew, it is another matter to persuade them to land.

For the Russian novelist Vladimir Nabokov (1899–1977), ideas are like butterflies: the talented thinker, like a skilful lepidopterist (which Nabokov also happened to be), must learn to lie patiently in wait until they can be coaxed into flying into the net of awareness.

For her part, the modernist writer Virginia Woolf (1882–1941) expressed intense jealousy at Marcel Proust's astonishing ability to catch so many butterfly thoughts and put into words the subtler concepts and tentative feelings that most of us register only in the outer airy zones of consciousness but cannot reach up to and turn into solid words:

Vladimir Nabokov:
catching a thought

Oh if I could write like that! [...] How has someone solidified what has always escaped – and made it too into this beautiful and perfectly enduring substance? [...] The thing about Proust is his combination of the utmost sensibility with the utmost tenacity. He searches out these butterfly shades to the last grain. He is as tough as catgut & as evanescent as a butterfly's bloom.

The core reason why we can't hold onto our bigger, more essential ideas is because, even though they are frequently crucial to our development, they also tend to induce intense anxiety. Just as a particular thought-bird or butterfly is about to settle on its perch or fly into our net, an alarm goes off in our minds: we panic, and the creature veers off at the last moment. We abandon our new train of thought and return to the comfort of more tamed, domesticated and familiar concepts.

We should not be surprised that thinking is so often interrupted by anxiety. New ideas threaten the mental status quo and are often sharply at odds with our existing commitments and habits. An original thought might, for example, alienate us from what people around us think of as normal. Or it might herald a realisation that we've been pursuing the wrong approach to an important issue in our lives, perhaps for a long time. One part of us may want the butterfly thought to elude us so we won't have to face up to a regret or loss. If we took a given new idea seriously, we might have to abandon a relationship, leave a job, ditch a friend, apologise to someone, rethink our sexuality or break a habit.

To encourage ourselves to know our minds, a blunt demand that we should 'think harder' may not be the best approach. In order to give new, threatening but important thoughts the best possible chance of developing, we may have to use certain mental tricks. The mind sometimes doesn't think too well if thinking is all it is allowed to do; it should be given a routine task to distract it and help it lower its guard.

For instance, a long journey alone in a train or on a plane, untethered from the distractions of our everyday lives, may render our minds more open to the consideration of disquieting ideas. The passing countryside gives us a spectacle to absorb our restlessness. Something similar might happen if we go alone to a café or take a walk in the countryside. The rhythm of our steps is semi-automatic; we half notice what's going on around us, but it's not important or urgent; the more paranoid, rigid surface of the mind can be gently occupied so that our deeper and more awkward thoughts can slip in unnoticed.

We should accept that our brains are strange, delicate instruments that evade our direct commands and are perplexingly talented at warding off the very ideas that might save us or help us flourish.

Mental Manoeuvre

1. It is normal to imagine that the best place to think would be a large room with a big desk, plenty of natural light and a window with a view. This is the premise behind the layout of most offices. The nearer one gets to the top, the closer one's workstation will approximate to this supposed ideal in tribute to the quality of thinking that one might do there.

2. But these assumptions are not true to the way our minds work. The primary obstacle to good thinking is not a cramped desk or an uninteresting horizon. It is, first and foremost, anxiety. The most profound thoughts we need to grapple with also have the most potential to disturb. If we were to pinpoint them accurately and get clear about their significance, we might need to make some big changes.

3. It is in this context that a shower emerges as one of the best places on earth in which to do any serious reflection. Amid the crashing water and the steam and with a few minutes of respite before the day starts, the mind is no longer on guard. We're not doing much inside our heads; we're mainly occupied with soaping our backs and rinsing our hair. The ideas that have been half-forming at the back of our minds – ideas about the true purpose of our lives and what we should do next – keep up their steady inward pressure, but now there

is less to stop them reaching full consciousness. We're not meant to be thinking and so – at last – we can think freely and courageously.

4. This quality of sufficient but not overwhelming distraction might equally well be present when we're driving down the highway or walking on a beach; when there's just enough for the timid, managerial side of the mind to be doing to keep it from interfering with our authentic and bolder inner machinations.

5. Our world places a high premium on good ideas but spends tragically little time planning how best to line up our minds to generate them.

4

Independent Thinking

From a young age, we are taught to expect that truly important ideas must lie outside of us; usually very far outside of us in time and place. Someone else – cleverer, wiser and more prestigious than us – will already have hatched the crucial thoughts; it is our task to pay homage to their intelligence, to learn what they had to say, to be as faithful as possible to their words and to align our perspective with theirs.

As part of this process, we will need to read a lot of books, listen to teachers and write untold numbers of essays about pre-existing intellectual authorities. We will find that the best way to convince anyone of anything we might be saying is to do our utmost to hide that we may have formulated the idea ourselves and instead to add copious footnotes to show that we got it all from someone else; preferably someone with a prestigious name and a long publishing record. One of the most foolhardy answers to any enquiry as to where a thought originated is to remark that it simply popped into our heads. Our heads are not understood to be where anything especially valuable might lie.

This readiness to submit to outside expertise has its merits: a society in which everyone refused to listen to those who had come before them would squander a lot of time, would be needlessly presumptuous and would have to keep reinventing wheels. But the background impulse automatically to mine the ideas of others before asking ourselves what we think is ruinous in its own way, leading to punishing degrees of stagnation, the wrong kind of conformity and a woeful number of minds that end up with their riches untapped.

Not all good ideas have yet been had, and our minds are as good a place as any in which they might one day hatch. We need to develop a greater loyalty to what is going on in these minds: we have met hundreds of people, experienced many places, entertained a vast variety of sensations and perceptions. Our minds are stocked. We have read more than Socrates; we have had as many – if not more – experiences than Plato. We don't have to go back to university to do yet another degree. We already have the raw material with which to produce valuable insights. We are simply lacking confidence.

One thinker who was especially irked by this tendency to underrate our own minds was the French philosopher Michel de Montaigne (1533–92). He took particular objection to the habit (already prevalent in his day) of manically footnoting and quoting other people in academic works:

> Whenever I ask an acquaintance of mine to tell me what he knows about something, he wants to show me a book: he would not venture to tell me that he has scabs on his arse without studying his lexicon to find out the meanings of scab and arse.

This kind of reluctance to trust our own experiences might not be problematic if other minds could be relied upon faithfully to express everything we have thought and felt; if, as it were, they knew all our arses and all our scabs. But, as Montaigne recognised, other people – even clever ones – will be silent on many important themes that circulate in our minds. If we allow existing thinkers to define the boundaries of our curiosity, we will needlessly hold back the development of our minds. A meeting in Italy crystallised the issue for Montaigne:

> In Pisa I met a decent man who is such an Aristotelian that the most basic of his doctrines is that the touchstone and the measuring-scale of all sound ideas and of each and every truth must lie in conformity with the teachings of Aristotle, outside of which all is inane and chimerical: Aristotle has seen everything, done everything.

Of course, Aristotle had done and seen a lot. Of all the thinkers of antiquity, he had perhaps been the most comprehensive, his works ranging over the landscape of knowledge. But the very scale of Aristotle's achievement bequeathed a problematic legacy. He had, paradoxically, prevented many of his successors from behaving like him, for he had risen to greatness only by doubting much of the knowledge that had been built up before him and putting immense faith in the fruits of his own mind.

Montaigne was criticising the impulse to think that the truth must always lie far from us, in another climate, in an ancient library, in the books of people who lived long ago. It is a question of whether access to genuinely valuable things must be structurally limited to a handful of geniuses born between the construction of the Parthenon in Athens and the sack of Rome, or whether, as

Montaigne daringly proposed, they might be open to you and me as well. He wanted to point us to an unexpected source of wisdom and insight: our own craniums. If we attend properly to our ideas and learn to consider ourselves plausible candidates for a thinking life, it is, implied Montaigne, open to all of us to arrive at insights no less profound than those in the great ancient books.

The thought is not easy. We are educated to associate virtue with submission to authorities rather than with an exploration of the volumes daily transcribed within ourselves by our perceptual mechanisms. Montaigne tried to return us to ourselves.

> We know how to say, 'This is what Cicero said'; 'This is morality for Plato'; 'These are the *ipsissima verba* of Aristotle.' But what have we got to say? What judgements do we make? What are we doing? A parrot could talk as well as we do.

Interesting ideas are, Montaigne insisted, to be found in every life. However modest our biographies, we can all derive greater insights from ourselves than from all the books of others:

> Were I a good scholar, I would find enough in my own experience to make me wise. Whoever recalls to mind his last bout of anger … sees the ugliness of this passion better than in Aristotle. Anyone who recalls the ills he has undergone, those which have threatened him and the trivial

incidents which have moved him from one condition to another, makes himself thereby ready for future mutations and the exploring of his condition. Even the life of Caesar is less exemplary for us than our own; a life whether imperial or plebeian is always a life affected by everything that can happen to a person.

It is only, proposed Montaigne, an intimidating scholarly culture that has made us doubt the rich insights of our own minds.

In the leading Italian novel of the 20th century, *The Leopard* by Giuseppe Tomasi di Lampedusa (1896–1957), one of the central passages describes two characters dancing together at a party, shortly after their engagement has been announced. They are in love but:

> ... they were blind to each other's failings, deaf to the warnings of fate, deluding themselves that the whole course of their lives would be as smooth as the floor they were dancing on. Neither was particularly kind, both were selfish, each had many secrets; yet there was something sweet about watching them together: their hopes were muddled and naive – but he was murmuring playfully in her ear; the scent on her hair was delightful; they were mortal creatures, for whom death was still an abstract, distant notion; they held one another, trying to brighten the brief passage between birth and death.

This paragraph is regularly held up to Italian students as a high point of literary brilliance. But there's a strange feature to it: there's nothing in it that we didn't already understand or know. The author did not have access to any truth from which we had been barred: we have seen couples dancing; we have been in relationships; we have experienced love; we know how complicated we are; we have had moments of tenderness and compassion for others despite their flaws. All the truths the passage describes were already in our minds, but we stayed silent. What might have held us back from writing similarly charming and true passages is that we have vastly under-respected our own intelligences: we have not had the courage of our most powerful intuitions. We have behaved as if we needed permission or a famous name like di Lampedusa, who was just like any of us until he started to take his own thoughts seriously.

Centuries earlier, the Italian Renaissance artist Michelangelo (1475–1564) had defined his own attitude to his work as a sculptor. 'The statue is already in the stone', he wrote, 'my work is to liberate it.'

Just like Michelangelo's stone, there are already all kinds of great thoughts in our heads: we merely need to liberate them from the inert block of our own hesitancy.

We suffer from excessive respect. We are taught to admire the minds of astonishing figures such as Michelangelo, Aristotle, Plato, di Lampedusa or Montaigne. We are invited to stand in awe at the achievements of these geniuses, but we are also made to feel that their thought processes must be quasi-magical and their ability to produce the ideas for which we know them ultimately mysterious.

But there is a radically different view, suggested by a prescient quote from the American writer Ralph Waldo Emerson (1803–82):

> In the minds of geniuses, we find – once more – our own neglected thoughts.

What this tells us is that the genius doesn't have different kinds of thoughts from the rest of us; they simply take them more seriously. We ourselves will often have our own sketchy, hesitant version of their ideas, which is why their works can have such a distinct impression on us. What they present feels surprising and impressive, yet also obvious and right, once it has been pointed out. They clearly and powerfully articulate notions that are already familiar to us because we've been circling them ourselves, possibly for years, without properly closing in on them due to our modesty.

In this sense, genius can be defined as paying closer attention to our real thoughts and feelings and being brave and tenacious enough to hold onto them even when they find no immediate echo in the world beyond. The reason why we disavow so much of what passes through our minds is under-confidence. We kill off our most promising thoughts for fear of seeming strange to ourselves and to others. This explains why small children are, in their own way, so much more interesting than the average adult: they have not yet become experts in what *not* to say or think.

Michelangelo, *The Awakening
Slave*, c. 1525-1530.

The point at which we censor and close down, when we take fright and try not to think, is exactly the moment when the so-called genius starts to take note of what is happening within them. We operate with a false picture of intelligence when we identify it too strongly with what is exotic and utterly beyond us. It is something more provocative than this. We can all be 'clever' when we truly attend to what is passing through consciousness. We all have very similar and very able minds; where geniuses differ is in their more robust inclinations to study them properly.

Mental Manoeuvre

1. Imagine, for once, that the truth does not lie outside of you.

2. Put aside external authorities.

3. Ask yourself what you think.

4. Stay faithful to what you have felt.

5. Believe that it is within your capacity to know.

6. Learn to catch your own unthought thoughts.

7. Examine – as it were – your own arse.

5
Focused Thinking

A central problem of our minds is that they tend to throw out thoughts that are vague. They aren't wrong, so much as imprecise – which means that we don't have a secure handle on what we truly feel or want and so are unable to steer our lives to accurate and satisfying destinations. The mind likes to point in general terms to sensations and wishes without delving into their specific characters. It spontaneously gives us the overall headline rather than the telling and operative detail, which means that we are hampered in our ability to formulate exact plans and to diagnose our real problems.

For example, when we are young and thinking about what sort of job we'd like to do, what may come to mind is that it should be 'creative' or involve 'working with people'. When we reflect on what's missing from our lives, we might point out a lack of 'fun'. Someone might ask us how we found a recent restaurant meal and we might capture our impressions with the term 'brilliant'.

Such accounts are not false, but they lack the specificity required in order to properly understand ourselves and our situation. To find the right sort of job, we need a more accurate grip on our talents and sources of satisfaction than is provided by the word 'creative'. Re-engineering our love lives will be difficult if the missing ingredient cannot be rendered any more precisely than an absence of 'fun'. Finding a meal 'brilliant' doesn't get us far in unlocking the secrets of successful restaurant visits.

To work against the inertia of the mind, we need to ask ourselves further questions. We need to break down our vague first feelings into their constituent parts: what is it about 'creativity' that we enjoy? During what moments of our current working lives do we feel dissatisfied? When we say 'fun', what do we really mean? What are five experiences of fun we might recently have had? And what are their opposites? We start with generalities and, if things go well with inner questioning, we end up with finely grained truths.

This is hard work. The first person to spot the arduousness, and to pioneer focused thinking, was the ancient Greek philosopher Socrates (c. 470–399 BCE). He became famous in Athens for standing around the marketplace asking what seemed like simple questions about what his fellow citizens were trying to achieve with their lives. They would tell him at once, and with great confidence, that they cared about 'justice' or that they admired 'courage' or that they were keen on 'beauty' or 'art'. Socrates would respond not by agreeing or disagreeing but by asking them what they meant by 'justice' or 'courage' or 'art' or 'beauty'.

These were not unfair questions: his friends were relying heavily on these words. But after a few minutes of more searching discussion, it would always turn out that these people couldn't say clearly what they meant. Socrates was getting at something fundamental: we go around feeling that our thoughts are clear, but if we submit them to further questioning, we realise that they suffer from a grave vagueness. However, there is no inner warning system to alert us to this; no intellectual alarm in our brains to shout 'watch out, you're being vague! You're formulating plans with woolly ideas!' We don't easily realise how out of focus our minds are and how at risk we will be of hitting reefs and shallows.

Vagueness is a problem because it means failing to pick out what really matters to us in any given situation. We might circle the right territory but we do not close in on the core issue, so our thoughts are ineffective guides to action. Suppose we like a film, but we can't really say why; when someone asks us, we can't define what's fascinating or impressive about it. Often this wouldn't matter. But if we're trying to become a cinematographer or scriptwriter, we won't know how to reproduce what has impressed us until we isolate what we really experienced.

In our thinking work, we are often like miners in search of a precious metal who initially always hit a compound ore; we need (without realising it) to sift out the valuable essence. Lack of a definition can sometimes seem like a purely academic worry, but it is at the root of many failed efforts and doomed goals.

Some of the big words and phrases that we rely on – like courage, love, justice, fun, art, family – are the deceptive public outer casing in which our own experiences, loves and fears are approximately contained. However, our own meaning is likely to be much more specific, more detailed and more intimate. To understand ourselves, we will need to discover, individually, the words that lie behind our first words.

The difference between vagueness and focus is what separates great from mediocre art. Marcel Proust had a friend, Gabriel de la Rochefoucauld, who wrote a novel called *The Lover and the Doctor*, which he sent to Proust in manuscript form with a request for comments and advice. 'Bear in mind that you have written a fine and powerful novel, a superb, tragic work of complex and consummate craftsmanship,' Proust reported back to his friend in his characteristically polite way. But the superb and tragic work had a few problems, not least because it was filled with clichés: 'There are some fine big landscapes in your novel,' explained Proust, treading delicately, 'but at times one would like them to be painted with more originality. It's quite true that the sky is on fire at sunset, but it's been said too often, and the moon that shines discreetly is a trifle dull.'

Why did Proust object? After all, doesn't the moon shine discreetly? Don't sunsets look as if they were on fire? Aren't clichés just good ideas that have proved rightly popular?

The problem with clichés is not that they contain false ideas, but that they are superficial articulations of very good ones. They are, to return to the crux of the issue, *vague*. The sun is often on fire at sunset and the moon discreet, but if we keep saying this every time we encounter a sun or a moon, we won't be getting at our actual sensations. When the first volume of Proust's novel was published eight years after *The Lover and the Doctor*, he also included a moon, but skirted ready-made moon talk in favour of an unusual and authentic metaphor that better captured the reality of the stellar experience:

> Sometimes in the afternoon sky, a white moon would creep up like a little cloud, furtive, without display, suggesting an actress who does not have to 'come on' for a while, and so goes 'in front' in her ordinary clothes to watch the rest of the company for a moment, but keeps in the background, not wishing to attract attention to herself.

A talented artist is, first and foremost, someone who takes us into the specifics of valuable experiences. They don't merely tell us that spring is 'nice'; they zero in on the particular contributing factors to this niceness: leaves that have the softness of a newborn's hands, the contrast between a warm sun and a sharp breeze, the plaintive cry of baby blackbirds. The more the artist moves from generalities to specifics, the more the scene comes alive in our minds.

The same holds true in painting. A great painter goes beneath a general impression of pleasure in order to select and emphasise the truly attractive features of the landscape: they show the sunlight filtering through the leaves of the trees and reflecting off a pool of water in the road; they draw attention to the craggy upper slopes of a mountain or the way a sequence of ridges and valleys open up in the distance. They've asked themselves with unusual rigour what is it that they particularly appreciated about a scene and faithfully transcribed their salient impressions.

The goal is not to become artists or philosophers, but to do something that accompanies these tasks: to move from woolly first impressions to authentic details; to go from vagueness to focus – and therefore to give ourselves the best chance of reaching what we actually seek.

_____ The difference between vagueness and focus is what separates great from mediocre art.

Mental Manoeuvre

1. Consider what you find exciting, desirable, beautiful or regrettable.

2. Note how the first answers are large and general, not so much wrong as vague, pointing to the general area without touching on live details.

3. Circle the vagueness and chip away at it (like Michelangelo with his hammer) with further questions:
- *What do you really mean?*
- *What is this unlike?*
- *When have you felt this before?*
- *How might you put this in different terms?*

4. What marks out good thinking is that it is precise. We start with ore; we should end up with a refined metal. We start with a block of stone; we should end up with a sculpture.

6
Philosophical Meditation

To understand ourselves, we need to take regular stock of the thoughts that flow through our consciousness.

Insofar as there is public encouragement of the idea, it tends to be according to practices collectively referred to under the term 'meditation'. In meditation, we strive to empty consciousness of its normal medley of anxieties, hurts and excitements and concentrate on the sensations of the immediate moment, allowing even events as apparently minor but as fundamental as the act of breathing to be noticed. In a bid for serenity and liberation, we still the agitations of what Buddhists evocatively term our 'monkey minds'.

But there is another approach to consider, based not on Eastern thought but on ideas transmitted to us via the Western tradition. In Philosophical Meditation, instead of being prompted to sidestep our worries and ambitions, we are directed to set aside time to catch, untangle, examine and confront them.

It is a distinctive quirk of our minds that few of the emotions we carry in them are properly acknowledged, understood or truly felt; that most of the thoughts that drive our behaviour exist in an unprocessed form within us. Philosophical Meditation seeks to lend us a structure within which to sieve the confused content that muddies our stream of consciousness.

Key to the practice is regularly to turn over three large questions.

What am I anxious about?
The first involves asking what we might be anxious about right now.

We are rarely without a sizeable backlog of worries, far greater than we tend consciously to recognise. Life, properly felt, is an infinitely alarming process even in its apparently calmer stretches. We face an assortment of ongoing uncertainty and threats. Even ordinary days contain concealed charges of fear and challenge: navigating through a train station, attending a meeting, being introduced to a new colleague, being handed responsibility for a task or a person, keeping control over our bodies in public settings – all contain the grounds for agitation that we are under pressure to think should not be taken seriously.

During our meditative sessions, we need to give every so-called small anxiety a chance to be heard: what lends our worries their force is not so much that we have them but that we don't allow ourselves the time to know, interpret and contextualise them adequately. Only by being listened to in generous, almost pedantic detail will anxieties lose their hold on us. At almost any time, a chaotic procession flows within our minds that would make little sense if recorded and transcribed: '... biscuits to the train why earrings deal they can't do it I have to Milo phone list do it the bathroom now I can't do, 11.20, thirty three per cent it a 10.30 tomorrow with Luke why invoices separately detailed why me trees branches sleep right temples...'

But such streams can gradually be tamed, drained, ordered and evaporated into something less daunting and illogical. Each word can be encouraged to grow into a paragraph or page and thereby lose its hold on us. We can force ourselves to imagine what might happen if our vague catastrophic forebodings actually came to pass. We can refuse to let our concerns covertly nag at us and look at them squarely until we are no longer cowed. We can turn a jumble of worries into that most calming and intellectually noble of documents: a list.

What am I upset about?

A Philosophical Meditation moves on to a second enquiry: What am I presently upset about? This may sound oddly presumptuous, because we frequently have no particular sense of having been upset by anything. Our self-image leans towards the well defended. But almost certainly, we are somewhere being too brave for our own good. We are almost invariably carrying around with us pulses of regret, loss, envy, vulnerability and sorrow. These may not register in immediate consciousness, not because they don't exist, but because we have grown overly used to no one around us giving a damn and have taken heed, along the course of our development, to recommendations that we toughen up.

Yet a life among others daily exposes us to small darts and pinpricks: a meeting ends abruptly; a call doesn't come; an anticipated reunion feels disappointingly distant; someone doesn't touch us when we needed reassurance; news of a friend's latest project leaves us envious. We are mental athletes at shrugging such things off, but there is a cost to our stoicism. From small humiliations and slights, large blocks of resentment eventually form that render us unable to love or trust. What we call depression is sadness and anger that have for too long not been paid their dues.

During a Philosophical Meditation, we can throw off our customary and reckless bravery and let our sadness take its natural, due shape. There may not be an immediate solution to many of our sorrows, but it helps immeasurably to know their contours. As we turn over our griefs, large and small, we might imagine we were entertaining them with a kind and patient figure who gave us the chance to evoke hurt in detail; someone with whom there would be no pressure to rush, be grown-up or impressive and who would allow us to admit without fear to the many things that have pained and reduced us in the previous hours.

What am I ambitious and excited about?

There is a third question we can consider within a Philosophical Meditation: What are we currently ambitious and excited about?

A part of our mind is forever forward-thinking and hopeful, seeking to maximise opportunities and develop potential. Much of this energy registers as vague tension about new directions we might take. We could experience this inchoate restlessness when we read an article, hear of a colleague's plans or glimpse an idea about next year flit across our mental landscape as we lie in the bath or walk around a park. The excitement points indistinctly to better, more fulfilled, versions of ourselves. We should allow our minds to wonder at greater length than usual about what the excitement (it could be a view, a book, a place, an insight) might want to tell us about ourselves.

In a poem written in 1908, the German poet Rainer Maria Rilke described coming across an ancient statue of the Greek

_____ It is a distinctive quirk of our minds that few of the emotions we carry in them are properly acknowledged, understood or truly felt.

god Apollo. It had had its arms knocked off at the shoulders but still manifested the intelligence and dignity of the culture that had produced it. Rilke felt an unclear excitement. He meditated upon and investigated his response, and concluded that the statue was sending him a message, which he announced in the final dramatic line of 'Torso of an Archaic Apollo':

> *Du musst dein Leben ändern*
> You must change your life

Influenced by German Romanticism, Rilke realised that he had fallen under the spell of an abstruse way of thinking and expressing himself. Now the Greek statue was being recognised by one part of his mind as a symbol of the intellectual clarity of ancient Greece, to which his conscience knew he needed to pay more attention. By decoding his excitement, Rilke was catching sight of an alternative way of being.

The case may be particular, but the underlying principle is universal. We each face calls, triggered by chance encounters with people, objects or ideas, to change our lives. Something within us knows better than our day-to-day consciousness the direction we may need to go in to become who we really could be.

A period of Philosophical Meditation does not so much dissolve problems as create an occasion when the mind can order and understand itself. Fears, resentments and hopes become easier to name; we grow less scared of the contents of our own minds, and less resentful, calmer and clearer about our direction. We start, in faltering steps, to know ourselves slightly better.

Mental Manoeuvre

1. Anxiety

Write down what you are anxious about; find at least eight things.
Each entry should be only a single word (or just a few words) at this point.

Don't worry if some of the anxieties look either trivial or dauntingly large. The mind tends to be an almost comedic blend of the two.
If you're having trouble, search for things that may be anxiety-inducing under the following categories:

- *Work*
- *Relationships*
- *Children/Parents*
- *Health*
- *Money*
- *Things I have to do*

Feel the curious release that can come from just making a list of these items. Huge relief can come from what we call 'unpacking' an anxiety. There are two kinds of unpacking we might do around any given anxiety.

There is **practical unpacking**: talk yourself through the practical challenge. Ask the following questions:

- *What steps do you need to take?*
- *What do others need to do?*
- *What needs to happen when?*

It is useful to have a calm and sympathetic part of yourself listening in on the detailed description of what needs to be done to address an issue. It's no longer merely an anxiety; it's a set of steps. They might not all be easy, but at least you are clearer about what they are.

There is also **emotional unpacking:** Talk yourself through an emotional challenge or set of doubts.

Describe the feeling in more detail. What do you feel it points to? Imagine trying to piece it together for a considerate friend.

The aim here isn't to solve all anxieties; it's to get to know them and to experience the relief that comes from clarity.

2. Upset
As quickly as you can and without bothering how petty, unreasonable or pretentious it might sound, write a list of current upsets; the more, the better. How have others hurt you? What are you sad, distressed, nostalgic or wounded about?

In the present safety of this exercise, allow yourself to be, for instance, furious about the way your partner brushes their teeth (too lackadaisical or too smug); the agents of global politics; your boss saying 'yeah, right' in a slightly sarcastic manner; the hotel receptionist who implied you might not be rich enough to stay there, or your mother commenting on your taste in shoes. These are just starting points; every starting point is valid.

Look at your list. Select two ways that people have hurt you that particularly preoccupy you, without considering the objective merits of your irritation. What is it about these things that bothers you? Go into as much detail as possible. Imagine you are pouring your heart out to a sympathetic and patient friend.

Now ask yourself: If this had happened to a friend, how would you advise them? What might you say?

Again, we're not attempting to resolve these issues as yet. The crucial issue is to get clear about what is actually distressing us. We're moving from vagueness to clarity.

3. Excitement

Rapidly list several things that have caught your attention and excited your interest since the last Meditation. A word or a brief phrase is sufficient for now.

Your list might (but doesn't need to) include:

- *Moments of envy – when you thought that someone else had something you might like to have a version of yourself.*
- *Daydreams: ideas about how life might ideally be, that you'd maybe feel awkward about telling others, because they might seem far-fetched, greedy or odd.*
- *How nice someone or something was.*
- *How thrilled someone makes you feel.*

Select two items that have particularly been on your mind. Pass them through a sieve of further questions:

- *Describe your excitement as if to a sympathetic, interested friend.*
- *If you could realistically change your life in certain ways, what would it be to change your life in the light of this?*
- *This exciting thing holds a clue to what is missing in your life; what might be missing?*
- *If this thing could talk, what might it tell you?*
- *If this thing could try to change your life, what changes might it advise?*
- *If other parts of your life were more like this, what might they be like?*

It would help if we could perform a Philosophical Meditation at least twice a week.

7
'Mad' Thinking

We banish many thoughts from our minds on the grounds that they are, as we put it, 'mad'. Some of them evidently are: too mean, flawed, absurd or petty to deserve further exploration. But it's one of the tragedies of our thinking lives that, amid the detritus of dismissed thoughts, there are invariably many that could have been of high value if only we had dared to examine them further; if only we hadn't been so scared of their less conventional and more speculative dimensions; if only we hadn't been so resistant to an occasional burst of 'mad' thinking.

Many of the greatest thoughts humanity has ever produced possess an unusual and, from some angles, insane dimension. The masterpieces of art, the business plans of certain corporations, the conversations of inspired lovers, the visions of political theorists, all have elements of protest against the settled status quo and contain aspects that are eccentric, contrary to received opinion and impatient with day-to-day practicalities – and yet have benefited our species. Our thinking lives are grievously harmed by a background imperative to appear at all times normal and sane. To maximise our insights, we should learn to make friends with moments of 'mad' thinking.

A central step in 'mad' thinking is to temporarily set aside the normal (but not always wise) restrictions on our imaginations. For instance, money is almost always a major consideration, but in a spirit of 'mad' enquiry, we can ask ourselves how we would approach an issue *if money weren't a factor.* Maybe we would suddenly see that a particular career deeply suited our nature; perhaps we would concentrate more on beauty or kindness, honesty or adventure; we might end up living in a different country or starting a new relationship.

Without the inhibiting need to think only within the parameters of sensible financial planning, ideas that we usually censor might come to the fore, some of which could be highly valuable. It could turn out, on closer examination, that some of our desirable plans were not entirely dependent on finances; it was simply that we had grown used to turning down more ambitious ideas on the grounds of money.

Similarly, around a career move, we could ask ourselves, in a 'mad' spirit, what we would do *if we knew we couldn't fail.* Liberated not to think always of our laughing critics, we might discover that we would like to pursue a business venture, if we knew it would be profitable after a few years; or perhaps we would concentrate on sport, if we were guaranteed to reach a professional level. We might spend more time looking after our children, if we knew this wouldn't prevent advancement in our working life. Or we might spend our evenings writing a novel, if we could be sure that it would get published and sell a respectable number of copies.

In reality, there can't be such guarantees, but holding our fears aside for a certain amount of time helps us to identify our areas of real enthusiasm, longing and ambition that we would otherwise push out of our minds too soon.

More broadly, we can use 'mad' thinking to develop our social and political perspectives. We might ask, for instance what our concerns would be *if we could be the absolute ruler of the world for a month.* Maybe we'd take interest in architecture or reinvent the school system. We might rethink how people get rewarded or whose face appears on magazines. We could redesign holiday resorts or re-engineer the way leaders are chosen. This 'mad' exercise helps us to recognise social and political ambitions that may have genuine merit. 'Mad' thinking is not, as we might first suppose, at odds with reality; it is an imaginative mechanism for revealing less obvious but important possibilities in the real world.

'Mad' thinking may not contain precise answers (how actually to remake the media or wean us off fossil fuels), but it encourages us in something that is logically prior to, and in its own way as important as, realistic solutions: the identification of a particular issue that we would like to see solved or that moves us.

Changes in personal life and in society and business rarely begin with practical steps: they start as a leap of the imagination, with a heightened sense of a need for something new, be this for an invention, a piece of legislation, a social movement or a new way to spend time with friends. The details of change may eventually get worked out, but the crystallisation of the wish for change has to take place at a prior stage, in the minds of people who can envisage what doesn't yet exist and isn't yet wholly reasonable.

One of the world's most inspiringly 'mad' thinkers was the French writer Jules Verne (1828–1905). In a series of novels and stories, he had the most unlikely thoughts about how we might live in the future. In *20,000 Leagues under the Sea* (1870), Verne narrated the adventures of the *Nautilus*, a submarine that tours the world's oceans often at great depth (the 20,000 leagues – about 80,000 kilometres –

Alphonse de Neuville and Édouard Riou, illustration from the 1870 edition of Jules Verne's *20,000 Leagues under the Sea*. 'Wouldn't glass shatter at that pressure?' We should keep certain questions at bay for long enough to shape a vision.

refer to the distance travelled).

When writing the story, Verne was not overly concerned with the technicalities of undersea exploration; he was more intent on describing the capabilities he felt such a craft would need. He described the *Nautilus* as being equipped with a huge window even though he had no idea how to make glass that could withstand immense barometric pressures. He imagined the vessel having a machine that could make seawater drinkable, even though the science of removing the salt from seawater had at the time hardly advanced. And he powered the *Nautilus* with batteries, even though this technology was in its infancy.

Jules Verne wasn't an enemy of technology; he was deeply fascinated by practical problems. But in writing his novels, he held off from worrying too much about the details to the 'how' questions. He wanted to create a vision of the way things could be, while warding off – for a time – the many practical issues that would one day have to be addressed. Verne was thereby able conjure the idea of the submarine into the minds of his readers decades before the technology emerged that would allow the reality to take hold. Eventually, we always need to work out answers to 'how' questions, but 'mad' thinking reminds us of the significance, dignity and legitimacy of starting with our intentions.

In his earlier story of 1865, *From the Earth to the Moon*, Verne had explored the notion of orbiting and then landing on the moon. He let himself imagine such a feat without getting embarrassed that it was entirely beyond the reach of all available technology.

Henri de Montaut, illustration for the 1865 edition of Jules Verne's *From the Earth to the Moon*. A concept could become real in part because it had first been imagined.

Verne imagined that the United States would launch a mission to the moon from a base in southern Florida. He fantasised that the craft would be made of the lightest metal he knew (aluminium). He assigned what seemed an unspeakably large price tag to the venture; the equivalent of more than the entire GDP of France at the time – which turned out to be a respectable guess at how much the Apollo programme would cost.

It was a truly prescient imaginative description. Verne's vastly popular book may not directly have helped any engineer, but it did something perhaps equally important: it fostered an aspiration. It explains why NASA named a large crater on the far side of the moon after Verne in 1961; the European Space Agency followed suit with the launch of the Jules Verne ATV, a spacecraft that travelled to the International Space Station carrying the original frontispiece of the 1872 edition of *From the Earth to the Moon* in its cargo bay.

Asking oneself to imagine what our lives might be like, without direct tools for a fix to hand, might feel immature and naive. Yet it is by formulating visions of the future that we more clearly identify what it is we might be missing, and so need, and thus set the wheels of change in motion. Through 'mad' experiments of the mind, we can counteract our debilitating tendency to squash our thinking around scenarios that might seem almost impossible. Such experiments are in truth often deeply relevant; when we look back in history, we can see that many machines, projects and ways of life that once appeared unfeasibly utopian have come to pass. Take for example, Captain Kirk's phone.

Captain Kirk's 'Communicator'
from the 1966 TV series of
Star Trek.

Mental Manoeuvre

1. In the privacy of the mind, allow yourself time for some 'mad' thinking.

- *What is the biggest version of your current ambitions?*
- *If you could not fail, what would you do?*
- *If others would never laugh, what would you do?*
- *If there were no financial pressures, how would you approach things?*
- *If you could be the absolute ruler for a while, how would you reform the world?*

Without thinking too much, complete the sentence: If I didn't have to be sensible, I would...

2. Describe your ideal country: What would the houses be like? What would the ideal corporation do? How would people have relationships? What technologies would they have?

3. Select a few bits of this madness – and make it your goal.

Etienne-Louis Boullée,
Cenotaph for Newton,
1784.

We all have a 'mad' side to our brains; we often keep it under wraps for fear of scorn or humiliation. Yet the road to many good ideas, precise insights and valuable suggestions has to pass through a few rather outrageous or ridiculous-seeming early notions. If we feel too much disgust or fear as our minds produce their wilder suggestions, we will stop the thinking process too early, and won't have given some of our best thoughts the chance they sometimes desperately need.

8
Friend Thinking

It is hard for us to think deeply and coherently for any length of time. We keep losing the thread. Competing, irrelevant ideas flit across the mental horizon and scramble our tentative insights. Every now and then, consciousness goes blank. Left to our own devices, we doubt the value of what we are trying to make sense of, and can experience overpowering urges to check the news or eat a biscuit. As a result, some of the topics we most need to examine – where our relationship is really going, what we might do next at work, how we should best answer a letter, what bothers us so much about the way our partner returns our hand after an attempt at a caress – founder, to our grave psychological cost.

What helps in our attempts to know our own minds is, surprisingly, the presence of another mind. For all the glamour of the solitary seer, thinking can sometimes happen best in tandem. The curiosity of someone else gives us the confidence to remain curious about ourselves. The application of a light pressure from outside us firms up the jumbled impressions within. The requirement to verbalise our intimations mobilises our flabby reserves of concentration.

Being a good listener is one of the most important and enchanting life skills anyone can have. Yet, few of us know how to do it; not because we are self-absorbed, but because no one has taught us how, and – a related point – few of us have been listened to sufficiently well. No wonder we come to social interaction hungry to talk rather than listen, eager to meet others but reluctant to hear them. Friendship degenerates into a socialised egoism. As is so often the case, this is reflected in our culture. Our civilisation is full of great books on how to speak – Cicero's *Orator* and Aristotle's *Rhetoric* were two of the most notable in the ancient world – but there is no equivalent landmark treatise on how to listen.

There are a number of things that the good listener does that makes it unusually nice to spend time in their company. Without necessarily realising it, our conversation with them often feels both urgent and exploratory. We're troubled at work; we're contemplating more ambitious career moves; we're not sure if our relationship is right for us; we are having family difficulties; we're worrying about something or feeling ground down by life in general (without being able to put a finger on exactly why); or perhaps we're excited and enthusiastic about something – though the reasons for our passion are tricky to pin down.

These are all issues in search of clarity. The good listener knows that, via conversation with another person, we'd ideally move from a confused, agitated state of mind to a calmer and more focused one. Together, through talking, we would work out what is really at stake. But, in reality, this tends not to happen because few of us are sufficiently aware of how to achieve this clarity from our conversation. There aren't enough good listeners. People tend to assert rather than analyse. They restate in many different ways the fact that they are worried, excited, sad or hopeful, and their interlocutor listens but does not help them to discover more.

Good listeners fight against this with a range of conversational gambits. They hover as the other speaks; they offer encouraging remarks; they make gentle positive gestures: a sigh of sympathy, a nod of encouragement, a strategic 'hmm' of interest. All the time, they are egging the other to go deeper into issues. They love saying: 'Tell me more about...'; 'I was fascinated when you said...'; 'Why did that happen, do you think?' or 'How did you feel about that?'

The good listener takes it for granted that they will encounter vagueness in the conversation of others. But they don't condemn, rush or get impatient, because they see vagueness as a universal and significant trouble of the mind that it is the task of a true friend to help with. The good listener never forgets how hard – and how important – it is to know our own minds. Often, we're in the vicinity of something, but we can't close in on what's really bothering or exciting us. The good listener knows we benefit from encouragement to elaborate, to go into greater detail, to push a little further. We need someone who will say two magic words: 'Go on...'

You mention a sibling and they want to know more. What was the relationship like in childhood? How has it changed over time? They're curious where our concerns and excitements come from. They ask things like: Why did that particularly bother you? Why was that such a big thing for you? They keep our histories in mind; they might refer back to something we said before and we feel they're building up a deeper base of engagement.

It's easy to say vague things: we mention that something is lovely or terrible, nice or annoying. But we don't really explore why we feel this way. The good listener has a productive, friendly suspicion of some of our own first statements and is after the deeper attitudes that are lurking in the background. They take things we say like, 'I'm fed up with my job' or 'My partner and I are having a lot of rows...' and help us to concentrate on what it really is about the job we don't like or what the rows might deep down be about.

They bring to listening an ambition to clear up underlying issues. They don't just see conversation as the swapping of anecdotes. Their approach to the chat you're having over pizza is allied with the philosophical ambitions of Socrates, whose dialogues are records of his attempts to help his fellow Athenians understand and examine their own underlying ideas and values.

A key move of the good listener is not always to follow every byway or sub-plot that the speaker introduces, for they may be getting lost and further from their own point than they would themselves wish. The good listener is helpfully suspicious, knowing that their purpose is to focus the fundamental themes of the speaker rather than veering off with them into every side road. They are always looking to take the speaker back to their last reasonable point, saying, 'Yes, yes, but you were saying just a moment ago...'. Or, 'So ultimately, what do you think it was about...' The good listener (paradoxically) is a skilled interrupter. But they don't interrupt to intrude their own ideas; they interrupt to help the other get back to their original, more sincere, yet elusive concerns.

The good listener doesn't moralise. They know their own minds well enough not to be surprised or frightened by strangeness. They know how insane we all are. That's why others can feel comfortable being heard by them. They give the impression they recognise and accept our follies; they don't flinch when we mention a particular desire. They reassure us they're not going to shred our dignity.

A big worry in a competitive world is that we feel we can't afford to be honest about how distressed or obsessed we are. Saying that one feels like a failure or a pervert could mean being dropped. The good listener signals that they don't see us in these terms. Our vulnerability is something they warm to rather than being appalled by. It is only too easy to end up experiencing ourselves as strangely cursed and exceptionally deviant or uniquely incapable. But the good listener makes their own strategic confessions so as to set the record straight about the meaning of being a normal (that is, muddled and radically imperfect) human being. They confess not so much to unburden themselves as to help others accept their own nature and see that being a bad parent, a poor lover or a confused worker are not malignant acts of wickedness, but ordinary features of being alive that others have unfairly edited out of their public profiles.

When we're in the company of people who listen well, we experience a powerful pleasure, but too often we don't realise what it is about what this person is doing that is so nice. By paying strategic attention to our feelings of satisfaction, we can learn to magnify them and offer them to others, who will notice, heal and repay the favour in turn.

Not every friend is a good thinking friend. They might be great fun to spend time with while being hopeless at teasing out our delicate, half-formed ideas. The good listening friend is loyal not so much to entertainment or anecdote, reminiscence or gossip; they are, above all, a friend to our still not fully developed ideas.

Mental Manoeuvre

Sit with a friend in a comfortable spot, with a clear stretch of time ahead of you.

One of you is in the listening role; the other in the speaker role. This can be reversed at another time. These are instructions for the listener:

1. Try not to interrupt the other person, to insert your own experience into the story or to feel pressure to come up with immediate sunny advice for them. Sometimes, what we most need is simply to feel heard.

2. When listening to something sensitive and painful, encourage your companion by looking interested, sympathetic and kind. You might at points just say 'hmm' – signalling interest and empathy, without saying anything that might inhibit or jar.

3. If you're listening and your companion recounts a lot of factual information while seeming to skirt any reference to their emotions (i.e. 'I got divorced and moved to a one-bedroom flat with good access to transport and quite large windows...'), try to direct them towards a more emotional layer. You might ask: 'How did that make you feel?'

4. When things get vague or unclear, ask: 'What do you mean by that exactly?' Make it obvious that there is no need for a brilliant definitive answer, just a little more clarification. It takes so much time to gather our thoughts and get them in order; the question can always be asked again.

5. If your companion recounts something clearly painful but doesn't appear to display much sympathy for themselves and appears keen to move on (i.e. 'My mum died when I was five but soon enough I was winning prizes at school...'), you might say an encouragingly kind word: 'That must have been very painful' – thereby giving them licence to feel an emotion they might have denied themselves.

6. If your companion answers the question very quickly and the silence is weighing, you might try a few smaller follow-up questions, such as:

- *Why do you think that might be?*
- *Can you say more about how that was for you?*
- *How did that leave you feeling?*

7. Sometimes, when people are about to answer a big question, they might say 'This must be so boring for you'. But perhaps what they really mean is that they are afraid of their vulnerability and are, indirectly, asking you to be especially sure not to get distracted when they feel so naked. Put their fears to rest and be sure to stay focused.

8. A lot of how we behave in the present relates back to things that happened to us in childhood. Treat the early period of life with particular curiosity.

9. We often suffer from shame; that is, a feeling that we're not good enough, that we are bad people, that we don't deserve things, that we're boring, ugly or unintelligent. It can be helpful to encounter a more forgiving, kindly, receptive person, who can hear us in our suffering and make us feel less alone. By letting your companion talk about what feels embarrassing or regrettable, you will be diminishing their sense of isolation.

10. Many of our problems have no concrete 'solutions'. Steer clear of any wish to find a practical answer at every point; this is not necessary and can even be unhelpful. Listening is of more value than advice. Often being heard with kindness will help someone come to their own solution.

Reverse the roles at different points in your friendship. We all benefit from speaking candidly and listening with care and love.

9
Reading Thinking

Reading has always had a central and prestigious place in our understanding of how we can develop our minds. The more we read, we're told, the cleverer we stand to be. We need to read because we can't do it all by ourselves; the fundamental point of reading is to acquire the good ideas of other people.

However true this might be, we can nevertheless point to another, perhaps less familiar, purpose to reading that is as important in terms of developing our minds: reading provides us with the chance to unearth and put into focus what we happen to think. It's through contact with the books of others that we might come to a clearer sense of our perspectives and ideas. The words of someone else can powerfully draw out our hitherto hesitant and disjointed notions; it is contact with another's intelligence that may bring our own thoughts into the light.

Even before we reach the specific content of a book, a basic benefit of happening upon a title that covers a topic we're interested in is that its existence provides an implicit endorsement of the thinking task ahead of us. In daily life, the people in our vicinity often don't want to reflect on exactly what concerns us at a given time; a topic we're curious about might be covered in just a few minutes at the table or dismissed as too complicated even to approach.

But when we find a book on the subject we care about but are lonely with, we have evidence of an extraordinary commitment made by a serious stranger, which bolsters our sense of the legitimacy of the thinking challenge we face. Someone else has devoted years of their life to our theme, and gathered 100,000 words in its honour – a devotion made all the more tangible by the gold lettering on the spine, the logo of a venerable publisher, the rich cream paper and an elegant blue bookmark.

Whatever might actually be inside, this is proof already that the thinking task is in principle a serious one; with this book in our lap, it no longer seems so peculiar to want to think in a sustained way about urban design or the future of marriage, child psychology or income differentials in developed countries. We are encouraged to start our own brains by evidence of the developed thoughts of another person.

Once we start to read the book, the benefit to our own train of thought continues. We're used to imagining that it's the ideas explicitly stated in a book that will enrich us, but we may not need the full thoughts of another person to come to a better sense of what we ourselves believe. Often, just a few paragraphs or even parts of sentences can be sufficient to provoke our minds and can nudge us to stop, daydream and reach for a notebook in which we jot down not the thought that we've read but the thought that it prompted inside us, which might be quite different and more significant. The book frames the topic for us; it puts the right question to us; it functions as the three dots that start us off ... and we do the rest.

Most valuably, we are privileged to disagree with a book, and are rewarded for doing so. Whatever the charms of an author with whose views we concur, nothing can quite beat the service sometimes paid to us by someone who we feel is tantalisingly off tangent; an author who starts to say something interesting, but then (in our eyes) goes off-piste; an author who hovers close to an essential point but then drops it in favour of something trivial, misguided or irrelevant. Assisted by the author's ploughing of the intellectual landscape, our personal thoughts can germinate in authentic and vivid directions. We put down the book and find a whole portion of our own thinking revealed to us. Our argument with the author powers our own reflections. By not saying what we quite wished to hear, the author brings us into newfound contact with what we actually believe and does us the service of releasing us from our intellectual under-confidence and languor.

The German philosopher Immanuel Kant (1724–1804) once credited the Scottish philosopher David Hume (1711–76) for teaching him how to think, but, in a nuance to the usual such tribute, added that Hume had done this not by lending him a set of ideas with which he could agree but by laying out with elegance and precision a whole class of philosophical positions from which he passionately dissented. Reading Hume's *Enquiry Concerning Human Understanding (1748)* had, said Kant, woken him from his 'dogmatic slumber' and inspired him to arrange his objections into what would turn out to be his masterpiece, *The Critique of Pure Reason* (1781).

We are so much the poorer if all we can do is agree with the books we read.

The role of books in reminding us of what we think through our inner arguments with them changes our sense of what an ideal curriculum might look like. It might include the sensible masterpieces, but there is good reason to find space in it for all the books that are fruitfully not very good or fascinatingly misconstrued or inspiringly erratic. When considered as a tool for thinking, so-called bad books might be just as effective as the acknowledged good ones – and sometimes a lot better; as we turn their pages, they allow us to imagine our own, superior versions of what we are taking in.

The practice of reading-thinking should be distinguished from reading-reading and venerated on its own terms. As we read, we should become interested not only in what the author says but, as importantly, in what we might think.

Mental Manoeuvre

1. While reading this book, don't pay too much attention to what is being said. Read only the first few paragraphs of any section, or even portions of sentences.

2. Use what is said here as an occasion to develop your own, superior ideas on effective thinking.

3. ...

10
Envious Thinking

We can start with two observations: firstly, it can be hard to know what we really want: what kind of relationship we're after; what sort of job would satisfy us; what we want our family life to be like. Secondly, we live in societies that take a dim view of envy: we're taught that the best thing we can do with envious feelings is never to experience them in the first place. Envy hasn't yet made its way into our register of experiences that we imagine could teach us anything.

However, if we could learn to handle our envy correctly, if we think it through with sympathy and skill, then it could play a key role in alerting us to what we genuinely want. Envious thinking can be the gateway to deeper self-knowledge and a profound understanding of our underlying ambitions.

We feel envy when someone else has access to an area of happiness that eludes us. The natural response to this feeling is shame; we feel we lack the generosity of spirit to celebrate their achievement. Perhaps we feel guilty for not sufficiently appreciating the lot we have. Yet envy, while uncomfortable, provides us with a message from confused but important parts of our personality about what we should be doing.

Experiencing the emotion of envy is uncomfortable, but squaring up to it is an indispensable requirement for determining our future: envy is a call to action. Without regular envious attacks, we couldn't know what we wanted to be and to have.

Instead of trying to repress our envy, we should examine it. Each person we envy is a piece of the jigsaw puzzle that is our future. There is a portrait of a 'true self' waiting to be assembled out of the envious hints we receive when we turn the pages of a newspaper or hear updates about the successes of old school friends or witness a friend's excitement about a new career move. Rather than run from the emotion, we should calmly ask one essential and redemptive question of all those we envy: 'What could I learn about here?'

Even when we do pay attention to the messages envy has to offer, we generally remain poor students of envy's wisdom. We envy certain individuals in their entirety, when, if we took a moment to analyse their lives, we would realise that it was only a small part of what they have or had done that really resonates with us. It might not be the whole of the café owner's life we want, just their skill at creating spaces in which people feel welcome. We might not truly want to be a painter, yet we might need in our working lives a little more of the playfulness on display in the work of one example we know. We are in danger of forgetting that the qualities we admire don't just belong to one specific, attractive life. They can be pursued in lesser, weaker (but still real) doses in countless other places, opening up the possibility of creating more manageable and more realistic versions of the lives we desire.

The problem with envy is its inaccuracy. Our impulse is to want the precise thing that another has, while in reality it is almost always only a bit that we need. The challenge isn't to avoid envy but to bring it more clearly into focus in order to guide our own next steps.

Mental Manoeuvre

1. Get a sheet of paper and divide it into four columns.

2. Title the first column on the left '*People I envy*': write a list of two kinds of people you envy – people from your life and famous people.

Include around six names, three of which you've heard about in the media and public life, and three people you yourself directly know, either well or just casually. Don't worry about the vagueness or peculiarity of the list. You might envy your sister, a guy you met for two seconds in a nail bar, or your own boss. Your list might look like this:

People I envy			
Steve Jobs			
Dr Dre			
Zadie Smith			
Yvonne			
Simone			
Mat's friend			

3. Now, in the column parallel to this, write down the achievements that they're most obviously known for.

People I envy	Their achievements		
Steve Jobs	iPhone		
Dr Dre	Beats		
Zadie Smith	*White Teeth*		
Yvonne	Private equity		
Simone	Printing press		
Mat's friend	Blogger		

4. Now go to the third column, which is trickier: here fill in something under the title '*The positive bits I don't really want*'. It's an odd but true thought: even when we envy certain people, it isn't the whole of them we actually envy. We don't mean that there are inevitably going to be some downsides to their lives. We mean that among the upsides, not all elements are going to appeal to us. So don't focus on the inconvenience of their job. Don't say 'the paparazzi' or 'the long hours'. Keep thinking of what is positive about their job/achievement but isn't actually for you.

People I envy	Their achievements	The positive bits I don't really want
Steve Jobs	iPhone	The management side
Dr Dre	Beats	The money
Zadie Smith	*White Teeth*	Fancy literature stuff
Yvonne	Private equity	Fancy coffee
Simone	Printing press	The content
Mat's friend	Blogger	The content

This can be surprising. It might be that when it comes to a really rich person, the thing you don't especially want is their wealth. Or with a creative person, maybe it's not actually the art you want. It could be something else: the capacity to manage your own time or the ability to use a foreign language.

5. Now it's time for the last column, titled '*The positive bits I want*'. This is the really precious part. It's different from the column titled '*Their achievements*'. The task is to evaporate from the very specific life you've found a few things that really interest you, a few moves that these people are making that lie at the root of your feelings of excited discomfort and painful longing.

People I envy	Their achievements	The positive bits I don't really want	The positive bits I want
Steve Jobs	iPhone	The management side	Marrying tech + beauty
Dr Dre	Beats	The money	Music + tech
Zadie Smith	*White Teeth*	Fancy literature stuff	Intelligent but cool
Yvonne	Private equity	Fancy coffee	Financial competence
Simone	Printing press	The content	Creative and lucrative
Mat's friend	Blogger	The content	Creative and lucrative

6. Use the bits of others' lives you truly seek to guide your next best efforts.

11
Analogical Thinking

One of the most striking capacities of the human mind is our ability to get clearer about ideas that might otherwise be vague or hard to grasp via a process of drawing analogies.

Analogy works by picking out a feature that is clear and obvious in one area and importing it into another field that is more confusing and intangible. Take the analogical phrase 'papering over the cracks', commonly used to suggest a shoddy, incomplete, lazy or dishonest manoeuvre. It is easy to develop a picture in our minds drawn from shoddy DIY of how putting up wallpaper can hide multiple defects in plasterwork. While it might be hard to see that, in a relationship, going on an expensive holiday won't do anything to address the daily conflicts of life together, or that, at work, moving to fancy offices won't alter the deep problems with the quality of the management team, bringing a vivid image from home decoration into the discussion can help to focus an issue in a relationship or in the workplace.

In the early part of the 20th century, while he was starting to write *In Search of Lost Time*, Marcel Proust was continually daunted by trying to find words to capture his sense of how multiple each of us is. So varied are we, he thought, it's almost as though every one of us contains multitudes, hiding under the cover of a single name.

One evening, Proust was sitting in a garden in Paris looking at a fountain: from a distance, it looked like a single column of water. But as he approached it, he saw that it was actually made up of lots of individual jets arranged closely together. It struck him that a good analogy for the aspect of human psychology he had been struggling to define would come from the Jardin du Luxembourg: we are each of us like a fountain, configured out of diverse, separate impulses, desires, attitudes and concerns that from a distance (seen by another person) give off an impression of being unified and coherent.

Analogies shed light not only on visual or psychological phenomena; they illuminate whole areas of intellectual concern. For example, in order better to understand what art is for, we might draw an analogy between art and advertising. We might say that a painting by Botticelli is a kind of advert for tenderness.

Thinking about art in terms of advertising helps us to see something that we might have missed if we had stuck more narrowly to an aesthetic lexicon: many works of art are trying to persuade us of something rather than just pleasing us; they are trying to seduce us to appreciate a particular point of view and want us to take their implicit philosophy deep into our souls. By drawing an analogy with adverts, which we know to be in the selling game, we can become newly conscious of the more didactic sides to certain paintings. We're not being sold products as such, but we are nonetheless being induced to 'buy into' attitudes and frames of mind.

Some of the best analogies function by illuminating an elusive area in one field with reference to a tangible and everyday one in another. When it comes to cooking, we know that a certain ingredient can be important in a dish even though it would be pretty useless on its own: for example, egg yolks play a crucial role in spaghetti carbonara, but a dish of only yolks would be unappealing.

This concept of one thing needing to combine with others in

Sandro Botticelli,
Madonna and Child,
c. 1470. An advert for
tenderness.

order to fulfil its potential value and of being unappetising in isolation is simple to understand in the kitchen, but it can be harder to grasp in other areas. For example, we often struggle to define what the role of money should be within a good relationship. Should it matter at all? Is it key? Should we even think of it? So we might reach for a cooking analogy: money is *one ingredient* in the dish of conjugal happiness, but a pure pile of cash on its own, without other ingredients (such as tenderness and generosity, self-knowledge and attraction) will be no more use than egg yolks without Parmesan cheese, pancetta, olive oil and spaghetti. An analogy is a deft mechanism for importing understanding from one region of our minds where it is in good supply to another where there is currently a shortfall.

It might seem to take a special type of imagination to come up with helpful analogies, and a rarefied degree of poetic genius to dream up the great literary comparisons, as when William Wordsworth (1770–1850) compared human loneliness to a solitary cloud drifting in the sky: 'I wandered lonely as a cloud.' However, helpful analogies are everywhere. It seems as if the universe is inherently structured as a set of motifs that repeat themselves across fields: the raindrops on a window will imitate the patterns of a dried-out river bed and the fissures on the surface of Mars will follow a similar logic as the lines on our palm.

This pattern repetition means that if we properly understand one aspect of one area, we already possess important clues for making sense of other aspects of other areas. What goes on in national politics will have close analogies with what typically happens in a relationship.

To understand a power struggle at the top of a large corporation, we might make a comparison with the machinations in a medieval royal court. The development of an adolescent can be illuminatingly compared to that of a frog from a tadpole. The behaviour of hormones in our bodies will follow some of the same patterns as air currents in the sky.

We are often more confused than we might be because we are brought up to think in silos. When things are unclear, we should look around for analogies from apparently alien but secretly sympathetic domains: biology should be invited to illuminate art, art politics, politics relationships, relationships nature, nature our moods, our moods cookery and so on.

The benefits of analogy form an argument for keeping our minds well stocked with knowledge from other disciplines, whatever domain we happen to be in. Engineers should spend time reading poetry, poets cookery books, cookery writers economics manuals and so on. When we are at moments of particular confusion, we should try to break the stalemate in our thinking by looking out for patterns, processes or phenomena in another subject that might bring clarity to our own. We stand to find a lot of lids that fit our respective jars.

Mental Manoeuvre

1. Try to describe a dilemma you are facing with different analogies from foreign disciplines.

2. Complete the following:
If my relationship were a car, it would be a...

....

If key people in my office were animals, they would be...

....

If my career were a kind of weather, it would be...

....

If the problem in my life was a moment in history, it would be...

....

If my body was a sort of material, it would be...

....

12
Empathetic Thinking

We're often in a position of needing to know what is happening in the minds of other people, whose thoughts and feelings we don't have direct access to. At work, we may have to imagine what our customers would like to buy more of from us; as a host, we may have to guess what our friends would like to eat or talk about; as a parent, we may have to picture what is happening in the mind of a pre-verbal child.

We tend to label the psychological capacity that allows us to penetrate the minds of other people in a remote way as *empathy*. It is via empathy that we'll be able to think our way into someone else's experience; that we'll be able to picture the desires and emotions of a stranger – and, in the process, make the world a more habitable place.

But how might we grow more skilled at empathy? It's typically assumed that the principal enemy of empathy is the ego; that what stops us from being able to read other people properly is a self-centredness and self-absorption. To nurture a more empathetic mindset, we should more often put ourselves aside, forget our ingrained way of seeing things and dissolve our habitual narcissism in order to enter into the foreign experiences of another being. The great enemy of understanding other people in this account is our excessive focus on ourselves.

However initially persuasive this thesis feels, it fails to diagnose what empathy truly involves. The way properly to enter the mind of another person is not to forget about oneself entirely; rather, it is to use one's knowledge of oneself to penetrate the consciousness of another. The best way to unearth the secrets of complete strangers is to look honestly into our own hearts.

What goes wrong in many attempts to read other people isn't that we're too focused on ourselves, but that we aren't bringing enough of our own experience to bear on another's unstated thoughts and feelings. We routinely end up displeasing or misreading others because we forget to apply our sense of what we want, feel, desire or worry about to a given situation. We imagine that other people are more alien than they actually are and cater to them accordingly, assuming that our knowledge of what we want to hear, to buy, to feel or to say won't be relevant.

Our lingering modesty has its origins in childhood. Growing up, it seemed inconceivable that a teacher who was three times our size and had a big beard might feel many of the same things we did, or that our father's boss or the mayor of the town could – beneath their forbidding appearances – be much the same as us. We assumed, from humility, that our fears and doubts, our silly moments, our hesitations and anxieties, our weirder thoughts and night-time desires had no corollaries in the minds and hearts of those older, wiser and cooler.

We tend to wall ourselves off like this because there's so little evidence that what we know goes on in our heads may also unfold in the heads of others. The grown-up world is painfully dishonest or at least edited, so it requires a leap of faith by us to dare to imagine that, despite evidence to the contrary, the most likely scenario is that the stranger will be like ourselves in most of the areas where it counts. When trying to work out what others want to eat, or what they might like to hear, or why they may be upset, the best move is to put our own ego into the picture, to imagine that our experience is relevant and that, despite the beard or different skin colour or gender or degree of wealth or geographical origins, what we're faced with is someone who is, first and foremost, a human like us.

When we're entertaining, for example, we often panic about what might please our guests. We imagine that we need to serve up something fancy and so rifle through cookery books we'd never use for ourselves. We forget to tap into the most powerful resource we have for serving a pleasing meal: our existing knowledge of what gives us pleasure when we're alone and peckish.

The last person we think of consulting is ourselves. We discard the claims of dishes we've reliably enjoyed for years, that we liked when we were twelve and still like now when we're on our own, assuming that others will be too sophisticated or too worldly to be charmed or delighted by something that is endorsed by our own humble experience. So, out of misdirected modesty, we cook a weird meat dish in an over-rich sauce from a venerable cookery book when we might all have been happier with fried eggs, toast and a few scoops of ice cream.

Becoming more empathetic will often involve going into the less familiar and sometimes less easy to accept parts of our own minds. The task of empathising with a thief, for example, can involve recognising our more expedient and compromised sides. Empathising with an unfaithful person will mean accepting our own buried promiscuous desires. The unempathetic person isn't usually selfish as not fully alive to the darker, more weird recesses of themselves; the parts that are a little criminal, or wild or vulnerable or sad. The opposite of empathy isn't just thinking of yourself; it's thinking of yourself in limited ways.

Understanding other minds will always be a hurdle, but we make it harder than we need to when we forget that the clearest guide to the secrets and psychology of strangers is that most unexpected source: ourselves.

Mental Manoeuvre

1. Other people are always likely to be more like you than like the alien, unfamiliar, puzzling people they appear.

2. In the absence of clear evidence, imagine that the other echoes your needs, fears, hopes and doubts. Use yourself as a guide to unlock the secrets of others.

3. With this in mind, think through some of the following scenarios:
- *What would it be nice to cook for guests?*
- *What would it be satisfying to talk about with a friend you'd like to get closer to?*
- *How might it be most reassuring to discuss sexual interests with a partner?*
- *What might your customers ideally want?*
- *What would be the best way to break the ice with a stranger?*

13
Death Thinking

One of the hardest things to think about with sufficient seriousness and intent is the meaning of our lives. We are generally too mired in the day to day, too pressed up against immediate deadlines, to be able to gain the altitude necessary to consider the course we are plotting through our ever more limited years; to ask ourselves with generosity but also rigour and impatience what we are trying to achieve in our careers or what kind of relationships we feel we should be in.

The major obstacle to rigorous thinking is the feeling that we are immortal. We may not experience ourselves as exactly this inured to the reality of death, but in the irresolute manner with which we approach the choices and hurdles before us, in the amount that we defer and evade, we are implicitly behaving as if this business of life, waking up each day, will go on forever. What other reason could we have for our failures to say what needs to be said, to square up to the challenges we have before us?

We are not terrified enough for our own good. We are behaving like gods or superhuman entities who have centuries to get it right. We are alternately too timid and too arrogant. We are ultimately simply scared; scared of doing something and getting it wrong, of making a decision and realising that it didn't improve anything. However, our inaction is also a form of choice, and not necessarily of the optimal kind.

To overcome our tendencies to delay and evade, we need to bring another, even greater, fear to the situation. We need to scare ourselves with something very large in order to spur ourselves to think with greater energy about the myriad challenges before us. That

Philippe de Champaigne,
Still-life with a Skull, circa 1671

is why, for hundreds of years, a key piece of interior decoration for any thinking person's study was a skull: a real-life skull with ghoulish eye sockets and irregular rotten teeth, so that as we went about our business, we would never be far from a reminder that our time was limited.

For much of our lives, however much the intellectual idea is in place, the reality of our own death remains in shadow: death is something that happens chiefly to other people. It's not a concrete, powerful conviction that shudders through us every hour. This not only allows us to keep unpleasant thoughts at bay and brings a touching innocence to our routines, but is also the breeding ground for the most unfortunate kinds of faulty thinking.

If we have more or less forever, we don't have to make any tricky changes or reforms. We can linger in a relationship that's not really working. We might waste many evenings half-heartedly amusing ourselves in trivial ways, imagining that we'll get around to more ambitious pursuits at some point in the future. Perhaps we don't have the kinds of friendships we'd really like, but we can live with the dissatisfaction out of a belief that we have decades still to get our interactions right.

The gruesome skull is meant to bring all such misplaced confidence to a conclusive end. It should also liberate us somewhat not to mind too much if we do hit obstacles in more ambitious ventures: if everything is doomed to end in the grave, then it might not matter overly if we were to approach an attractive stranger and be rebuffed, or if we tried our hand at a new task and discovered that we had no talent. While the thought of death may be terrifying, its inevitability might also usher in a feeling of fruitful experimentation.

A picture of us from our childhood could be the ideal companion to this skull. When we were little, we had no sense that we might be an adult one day. At five, turning twenty or thirty was an impossible supposition. Yet it has happened sure enough. And just as this has come to pass, so our death will happen too. The childhood picture and the skull combine to force the reality of our end powerfully to the front of our recalcitrant brains, not to make us miserable but to render us more active, strategic, focused and determined in the precious present; in short, to help to save us.

Mental Manoeuvre

1. Go online and look up the death clock, which will inform you of how many days and seconds you (statistically) have left.

2. While the clock is ticking, consider your existence with new energy. Ask yourself:

- *What sort of a relationship would you like to have?*
- *What parts of the world would you like to see?*
- *What kind of job is fit for your talent?*
- *What is your mission and purpose?*

14
Love Thinking

One of the great intellectual puzzles that daily life forces us to consider on a regular basis is: 'Why are other people so awful? How come they are so unreliable, aggressive, deceitful, mean, two-faced or cowardly?' As we search for answers, we tend to fall back on a standard, compact and tempting explanation: because they are terrible people. They are appalling, crooked, deformed or 'bad'; that's simply how some types are. The conclusion may be grim, but it also feels true and fundamentally unbudgeable.

However, when things feel especially clear-cut, we may be goaded to try out an unusual thought experiment, which stands to challenge many of our certainties and render the world usefully more complicated: we can try to look at our fellow humans through the eyes of love.

The experiment requires particular stamina and is best attempted at quieter, less agitated times of day. When we manage it, it may count as one of our highest ethical achievements.

We are normally resolutely on our side, deeply invested in our own point of view and prone to trade in settled and moralising certainties. Yet occasionally, we have the strength to look at other people through a different lens: we notice that their reality is more complicated and nuanced than we first expected and that, contrary to our impulses, they may be deserving of more sympathy and consideration than we supposed, even though they have hurt and frustrated us, even though their behaviour runs contrary to what we expect, and even though the temptation has been to call them idiots and numbskulls and move on.

Looking at another person through the eyes of love involves some of the following:

Imagination

Moralistic thinking identifies people closely with their worst moments. Love thinking pushes us in another direction: it bids us to use our imaginations to picture why someone might have done a regrettable deed and yet could remain a fitting target for understanding and sympathy. Perhaps they got frightened; maybe they were under pressure of extreme anxiety and despair. They might have been trying to say or do something quite different, and this was all they could manage.

Those who look with love guess that there will be sorrow and regret beneath the furious rantings or a sense of intolerable vulnerability behind the pomposity and snobbishness. They will intimate that early trauma and let-down must have formed the backdrop to later transgressions. They will remember that the person before them was once a baby too.

The loving interpreter holds on to the idea that sweetness must remain beneath the surface, along with the possibility of remorse and growth. They are committed to mitigating circumstances and to any parts of the truth that could cast a less catastrophic light on folly and nastiness.

Hurt, not bad

Love thinking refuses to believe that there is anything such as evil pure and simple. Bad behaviour is invariably the consequence of hurt: the one who shouts did not feel heard; the one who mocks was once humiliated; the constant cynic had hope snatched from them. This is not an alternative to responsibility; it is a rightful awareness that acting badly is invariably a response to a wound and never an initial ambition.

The fundamental step of love is to hold on, in challenging situations, to a distinction between a person's overt unpleasant actions and the sympathy-worthy motives that underlie them.

A story, not a headline

Moralistic thinking likes headlines; love thinking goes in search of stories. 'Angry spouse abandons family' will have its origins decades before, in the old house, at the hands of unsteady parents, when innocence was first lost and stability destroyed. 'Scandalous CEO ruins company' isn't a story of greed or venality, but one of confusion and mental illness. In the face of caricature, the task of love is adequate curiosity.

The child within

To consider others with love means forever remembering the child within them. Our wrongdoer may be fully grown, but their behaviour will always be joined up with their early years. We're so keen to treat others like the adults they are that we overlook the need occasionally to perceive, and sympathise with, the angry and hurt infant lurking inside.

When we are around small children who frustrate us, we

don't declare them evil; we don't bear down on them to show them how misguided they are. We find less alarming ways of understanding how they have come to say or do certain things. We don't readily assign a negative motive or mean intention to a small person; we reach around for the most benevolent interpretations. We probably think that they are getting tired, or their gums are sore, or they are upset by the arrival of a younger sibling. We have a large repertoire of alternative explanations ready in our heads.

This is the reverse of what tends to happen around adults; here we imagine that others have deliberately got us in their sights. But if we employed the infant model of interpretation, our first assumptions would be quite different. Given how immature every adult necessarily remains, some of the moves we execute with relative ease around children must forever continue to be relevant when we're dealing with another so-called grown-up.

The possibility of tragedy

Moralistic thinking is sure that people get what they deserve. Love thinking believes in the existence of tragedy; that is, in the possibility that one can be good and still fail. Tragedy teaches us that the most shocking events can befall the more or less innocent or the only averagely muddled and weak. We do not inhabit a properly moral universe; disaster is at points distributed unfairly to those who are wholly undeserving. Love thinking accepts a remarkable, frightening and still-too-seldom-accepted possibility: that failure is not reserved for those who are 'evil'.

Patience

Moralistic thinkers reach their certainties swiftly; love thinkers take their time. They remain serene in the face of obviously unimpressive behaviour: a sudden loss of temper, a wild accusation, a mean remark. They reach for reasonable explanations and have in their minds the better moments of a currently frantic but essentially loveable person. They know themselves well enough to understand that abandonments of perspective are both normal and usually indicative of nothing much beyond passing despair or exhaustion. They do not aggravate a febrile situation through self-righteousness – a symptom of not knowing oneself too well and of a selective memory. The person who bangs a fist on the table or announces extravagant opinions is most likely to be simply worried, frightened, hungry or just enthusiastic; conditions that should invite sympathy rather than disgust.

Redeeming features

Love thinkers interpret everyone as having strengths alongside their obvious weaknesses. When they encounter these weaknesses, they do not conclude that this is all there is; they know that almost everything on the negative side of a ledger could be connected up with something on the positive. They search a little more assiduously than is normal for the strength to which a maddening characteristic must be twinned.

We can see easily enough that someone is pedantic and uncompromising; we tend to forget, at moments of crisis, their thoroughness and honesty. We may know so much about a person's messiness, we forget their uncommon creative talent. There is no such thing as a person with only strengths, but nor is there someone with only weaknesses. The consolation comes in refusing to view defects in isolation. Love is built out of a constantly renewed and gently resigned awareness that weakness-free people do not exist.

We are sinners too

The single greatest spur towards a loving perspective on others is awareness that we are also imperfect. The enemy of generosity is the sense that we might be beyond fault, whereas love begins when we can acknowledge that we are in equal measures idiotic, mentally wobbly and flawed. It is an implicit faith in their own perfection that turns people into unbearably harsh judges.

Looking at the world through the eyes of love, we conclude that there is no such thing as a simply bad person, and no such thing as a monster. There is only ever pain, anxiety and suffering that have coalesced into unfortunate action. This isn't merely an exercise in being nice; it's an exercise in getting to the truth of things, which may, when we get down to the details of human psychology, be roughly the same thing.

Mental Manoeuvre

1. Think of the most 'awful' people in your orbit:
- *one who shouts a lot*
- *one who is bitter*
- *someone who hugely inconvenienced everyone*
- *you when you hate yourself*

2. Apply love thinking; and see humans emerge from monsters.

15
Sceptical Thinking

One of the stranger moves we all have to practise if we are to learn to think effectively is more regularly to imagine that we might be wrong. The good thinker is, to a large extent, first and foremost a *sceptic*.

Scepticism began as a polemical philosophical movement in ancient Greece in the 4th century BCE (so named after the Greek word *skepsis*, meaning questioning or examination). It concentrated on showing up how unreliable our minds could be, in both large and small ways. Pyrrho, the plain-speaking founder of the sceptical movement, liked to point out that the average pig is cleverer, sharper, kinder and happier than its human counterpart.

The sceptics identified a range of cognitive malfunctions and blind spots that afflict our species. We are notoriously bad judges of distances, they argued, wildly misreading how far away a distant island or mountain might be, and easily fooled in our estimations by small changes of light and moisture in the air. Our sense of time is highly inaccurate, influenced chiefly by the novelty or familiarity of what happens rather than by its strict chronological duration. We desire excessively and inaccurately. Our sexual drives wreak havoc on our sense of priorities. Our whole assessment of the world can be transformed according to how much water we have drunk or how much sleep we have had. The instrument through which we interpret reality, our 1260 or so cubic centimetres of brain matter, has a treacherous proclivity for throwing out faulty readings.

For the sceptics, understanding that we may be repeatedly hoodwinked by our own minds is the start of the only type of intelligence of which we are ever capable; just as we are never as foolish as when we fail to suspect we might be so.

We take the first steps towards effective intelligence by determining some of the ways in which our minds deny, lie, evade, forget, obsess and steer us towards goals that won't deliver the satisfaction of which we're initially convinced. A readiness to mitigate the worst of our everyday foolishness contributes to the highest kind of intelligence of which we may ever be capable.

Part of thinking effectively is knowing, at one level, the likelihood that we might not be thinking well and so proceeding with humility and an appreciation of our mind's characteristic tricks: this mind may be tired but unaware that it is so; it may be under the sway of emotion but certain it is calm; it may be judging a situation in the present according to a bias unconsciously picked up in childhood.

Thinking well means trying to put in place measures that can mitigate for the worst of our tendencies: always sleeping on a major decision; always ensuring that we have had enough food and water when we are reflecting hard; always trying to make a case for the opposite point of view to the one we're initially and emotionally attracted to; always questioning our feelings rather than submitting to their excitements.

A commitment to scepticism will affect how we behave around others. The non-sceptical person has a high degree of faith in their ability to judge relatively quickly and for the long term what is right and wrong about a given situation. They feel they can tell who has behaved well or badly or what the appropriate course of action should be around a dilemma. This is what gives them the energy to get angry with what strikes them as rank stupidity, or to blow up bridges with people they've become vexed with, or to state a disagreement emphatically and to call another person stupid, monstrous or a liar to their face. Once they have said something, they know they can't take it back, but they don't really want to. Part of their frankness is based on the notion that they can understand at speed the merits of any situation, the character of others and the true nature of their own commitments.

The sceptical person has learnt to be careful on all these fronts. They are conscious that what they feel strongly about today might not be what they think next week. They recognise that ideas that sound strange or misguided to them can be attempts to state – in garbled forms – concepts that are genuinely important to other people and that they themselves may come around to with time. They see their own minds as having great capacities for error and as being subject to imperceptible moods that will mislead them, and so are keen not to make statements that can't be taken back or to make enemies of people they might decide are worthy of respect down the line.

The sceptical person will be drawn to deploying softening, tentative language and holding back on criticism wherever possible. They will suggest that an idea might not be quite right. They will say that a project is attractive but that it could be interesting to look at alternatives as well. They will consider that an intellectual opponent may well have a point.

They aren't just lying or dodging tough decisions. Their behaviour is symptomatic of a nuanced and intelligent belief that few ideas are totally without merit, no proposals are completely wrong and almost no one is entirely foolish. They work with a conception of reality in which good and bad are entangled and in which parts of the truth are always showing up in unfamiliar guises in unexpected people. Their politeness and hesitancy is a logical, careful response to the complexity they identify in themselves and in the world.

We will have learnt to be good sceptics, and better thinkers, when we always maintain a position of doubt with regards to the troubling and devilishly unreliable tool with which we're trying so hard to think well.

Mental Manoeuvre

1. Imagine, always and sincerely, that everything you believe to be right might be wrong.

2. Sleep on decisions; never be too certain; distrust your own mind. Stay alive to the momentous impact of low blood sugar on any idea.

3. Build a broad margin of error into every thinking move you make.

The School of Life
for Business

These essays are thought pieces based on the topics covered by The School of Life for Business. We teach twenty emotional skills to help businesses thrive in the modern economy. We work with businesses to help employees function better together – to form more engaged teams, be more productive, dynamic, and work together in more innovative and entrepreneurial ways. We build emotional skills programmes for each organisation we work with, delivered by a world class faculty.

For more information, see:

www.theschooloflife.com/business

List of works

P15
Fra Angelico, *Crucifixion with Saints (detail: head of St. Benedict)*, 1441. Fresco, 550 cm x 950 cm. Convento di San Marco, Florence.

P23
Marcel Proust, *In Search of Lost Time autograph manuscripts.*
© Bibliothèque nationale de France, Paris.

P43
Michelangelo, *The Awakening Slave*, 1525-1530. Marble sculpture, 267 cm. Florence, Italy. © 2019 Photo Scala, Florence.

P61
"Archaic Torso of Apollo" translation copyright © 1982 by Stephen Mitchell; from SELECTED POETRY OF RAINER MARIA RILKE by Rainer Maria Rilke, edited and translated by Stephen Mitchell. Used by permission of Random House, an imprint and division of Penguin Random House LLC. All rights reserved.

P71
Alphonse de Neuville and Édouard Riou, Illustration of the *Nautilus*, *20,000 Leagues Under the Sea*. Chronicle / Alamy Stock Photo.

P73
Space capsule manoeuvering ready for Moon landing. From Jules Verne "Autour de la Lune", Paris, 1865. Wood engraving. Photo 12 / Alamy Stock Photo.

P77
Étienne-Louis Boullée, Cénotaphe à Newton, 1784. Art Collection 2 / Alamy Stock Photo.

P106
Sandro Botticelli,
Madonna and Child, circa 1470.
Tempera on panel, 74.5 cm x 54.5 cm.
National Gallery of Art, Washington,
D.C.

P119
Philippe de Champaigne,
Still-life with a Skull,
vanitas painting, circa 1671.
Oil on panel, 28 cm x 37 cm.
Musée de Tessé, Le Mans, France.

Picture credits

To join The School of Life community and find out more, scan below:

The School of Life publishes a range of books on essential topics in psychological and emotional life, including relationships, parenting, friendship, careers and fulfilment. The aim is always to help us to understand ourselves better and thereby to grow calmer, less confused and more purposeful. Discover our full range of titles, including books for children, here:

www.theschooloflife.com/books

The School of Life also offers a comprehensive therapy service, which complements, and draws upon, our published works:

www.theschooloflife.com/therapy